Be Powerfully You

Janet

WHERE'D MY CONFIDENCE GO...

and how can I get it back?

Janet Zaretsky

Janet Zaretsky RN ret., CPBA, CPMA,
Enhanced C-IQ Coach,
Master Business Coach
512-553-2927
Janet@JanetZaretsky.com
www.JanetZaretsky.com

Acknowledgments

The completion of this book happened because of the amazing life I have led and the special people who have contributed to me and my life. First, my husband, Lee Zaretsky, who has always been my biggest supporter. To be married to a man like Lee, who is always there and steadfastly backing me allows me to be in the world contributing at a level I never knew I could. Then, of course, my daughters, Kristen and Erica; raising each of them under different living conditions and circumstances allowed me to grow as a human being and they are both amazing young women in their own right.

I started my career as a Registered Nurse because I loved science and the person I most admired was my mom, who was an RN. I lost her when I was only 29, but the courageous outspoken woman she was groomed me to be who I am. I miss her always and am grateful to her and my dad for my life, my love of education and for the amazing people whom I have in my life.

I acknowledge Coach University for starting me on a path that would lead me to my life's passion. I have had great teachers and coaches along the way, including Judith Glaser, who opened up the world of neuroscience and coaching to me. Lastly, I acknowledge and appreciate Landmark Worldwide for the opportunity to lead programs and develop myself to be someone who makes a profound and lasting difference in the world.

It is with gratitude and a commitment to contribute to the quality of the lives of the people for whom I wrote this book. It is my wish that this book contributes to your life, dear reader.

My Commitment to You

Reading this book will make a difference for you and elevate your confidence. I have created a bonus workbook to maximize finding your confidence and restoring you to maximum power.

This free download is available at:
http://www.wheredmyconfidencego.com

Table of Contents

Where Did My Confidence Go?

I ran breathlessly up that hill and proclaimed proudly, "I am king of the hill!" I had finally done it. I had fought hard and bested my three brothers to take the hill. I was eight years old and the second child of five boisterous children. We were less than two years apart. We played outside in our suburban Dayton, Ohio home on most days (*I suspect my mom wanted all that noise somewhere else!*). To this day, when we are all together, now with our own families, and our parents no longer alive, it is still noisy with every one of us trying to get heard, trying to get noticed; trying to take that "hill."

Like all kids, I was confident I could do anything I wanted and would work long and hard to win. The times when I didn't win served as fuel for the next attempt. In my memory, winning that hill, declaring myself King of the Hill, was such a vivid moment of triumph because I had been trying to win "forever!" When you have three brothers, who band together against you, it is not an easy feat to win. And "I will win" was my attitude back then. *Until life happened.*

As all of us know, as we get older and our work is not to "play in the neighborhood," everything gets more complicated. Life is no longer a win/lose proposition. We often have more than three brothers banded together against us. Losing and winning doesn't end up in wild laughter and abandon. Life, it seems, gets serious and significant.

Life seems to hand us lessons, and often, with those lessons, comes the loss of many things. We lose that naivety of youth, the exuberance of games, and all too often, we misplace important things like our confidence and our power. We begin to step over small things, "going along to get along, "which often comes back to bite us; further undermining our power!

Did you ever wonder, "Where did my confidence go?" You once were confident, like me, declaring "I am King of the Hill!" and now, here you are, at whatever age you are, questioning yourself and playing it safe. Where did it go? And more importantly, how can you find it again?

That is what this book is about. You and I are going to find your confidence, get you back to your full power; you and I, together!

*You **are** King of the Hill!*

---------------- CHAPTER I ----------------

The Magical Ingredient... Confidence!

It all comes down to confidence. I know it may not seem like it. You may have lots of other explanations for why you are not fully satisfied, not happy, not as successful as you want to be, not making the money you want, but the explanations are... well, wrong.

I know you might want to argue about this with me and this seems like a strange way to start a conversation – having you already resisting what I have to say; however, if you will just stick with this conversation, I promise you, it *will* be worth it.

I know you are reading a book, but to me, I am having a conversation with you. We are sitting down and talking. I may not know you personally, but **I do know you.** *You are someone committed to your own success and greatness. Here is what I want you to know about me – I am committed to that, too! So, let's talk!*

The question to ask is; Where did your confidence go? You, like me, were full of confidence when you were young. It is likely that you thought you could do, and be, anything you wanted.

You might not remember being full of confidence. However, you were. Really.

I have worked with thousands and thousands of people and some remember when they lost their confidence and some don't. It is all fine. Let's just talk about it.

Did you want to be an astronaut, or a dancer, or a mom, or the President of the United States? What was your dream?

I wanted to be a veterinarian, an architect, a doctor, a nurse, a school teacher, and even an astronaut. I dreamt about having a ton of dogs and horses. I wanted to be a nurse like my mom, and later, a doctor. I loved my teacher in elementary school and thought it would be so much fun to be in the front of a classroom and have everyone listen to me! I loved life; I loved learning, and everything seemed so possible and so available to me.

When I was in fourth grade, I gave a speech, and received a ton of praise for that speech. I don't remember what it was about; just that I loved fourth grade and I knew I wanted to write, speak, and travel. I always spoke up, I won speech contests. I wrote stories and received great feedback and got the message that I was good! Hey, who doesn't like being admired? I sure do! Then, off I went to high school, all full of confidence. I was so sure of myself, I enrolled in a sophomore level speech class, as a freshman. I was pretty proud of myself and, as was customary, was getting good grades.

Since you don't know me well, I also must tell you that I was (and still am) a bit of a rebel. I am not great at following rules, unless I agree with them, of course!

Well… one of the rules in speech class was "no chewing gum." I did not agree with that rule. Here is what I remember: One day I was sitting in class, and was chewing gum and suddenly, I got caught. My punishment was to stand in the front of the class with gum on my nose. I was humiliated; and, as is common with teenagers, I was teased mercilessly. I could not handle that, so I dropped out of the class.

Speaking in public… that dream? Killed off in that one incident. Done. Later, when I was a nurse for the state of California, I was the chairperson of a fundraiser and I was called to the front of the room to be recognized. I remember vividly turning to my boss, Sue, and saying "I hate speaking in public." I then walked to the raised platform and tripped… falling flat on my face; literally splayed out, face down. I sat up, and laughed with everyone else, like any "good sport" would do; but, inside, that one incident sealed the deal for me. Oh, yes, I hated speaking in public! Zero confidence. Fear, trepidation, and the true probability of humiliation replaced all my confidence.

Here is what I want you to know. I *am* a public speaker. I have been speaking in public for 21 years now, and I have spoken in front of rooms with hundreds of people in attendance. People pay to hear me speak. I have given talks to thousands and thousands of people. I am sought after, as a speaker and, I am really really good at it! No fear, no trepidation... just confidence. And the concern about humiliation? Gone... *really, gone.*

I have even had some funny incidents: Once, as I led a class, I was standing on an elevated platform. There were about 100 people there. I was talking with my hands, as usual, and all of the sudden I felt a breeze.

I looked down and all of my buttons, except the top one, had come undone on my blouse. I said, "Excuse me," turned around and buttoned my blouse. I then asked the audience, "How long has my blouse been unbuttoned?" to which they replied, "About an hour." I asked, "Why didn't you tell me?" to which they said, "We did not want to embarrass you!" – to which I replied, "You mean as opposed to me standing here with my belly and bra showing? – OMG!" I joked, and moved on.

Oh yeah, my confidence, my "mojo" was totally back! I know, you want to know how I got my mojo back. Later, my friend, I will tell you, I promise.

That is a bit of one of my stories. I will share more of them as we talk further. And I will share specific stories of some of the amazing people I have coached through these past 21-plus years.

Why I am saying to you that it all comes down to confidence is because in coaching thousands of people, I have seen the theme. It doesn't seem like it is confidence. It may seem like the issue you don't feel powerful in is money, or communication or time management or delegation or something else, but what is underneath that is some lack of confidence. Let's look together.

I am having this conversation with you so that you, too, can climb the pillars of power and get your confidence back **fully** and get what you want in life and in your business or career.

One thing I have noticed is that when you assess what your experience is, you will find what is weak. When you know your weaknesses, you can take action to make the area that is weak, stronger.

As we go along, I invite you to really look, and assess, all the areas in life where you notice weakness – so that you can take action and GET YOUR MOJO back! Be as honest as possible – and, remember, no one is looking but you!

15 - Clarity → willingness → Killing alternatives
   (Risky)

CHAPTER 2

There is No Gold at the End of that Rainbow!

Why have clarity? Because, when you have clarity, you are vitally aware of your value. How does that show up? You ask for the salary you know you are worth, or get paid the fees for the service you provide and you are paid well for those services. You don't back down when someone questions you. You don't step over things that do not work well for you. When asked what you do, you state what you do for a living in a confident tone with a description that conveys your power and worth; no hesitation. You are not self-deprecating. You experience being solid, grounded, and you are not searching for the next "right" thing. You wake up in the morning and execute whatever you had planned to do, with purpose. You don't regularly procrastinate. You know who you are and are being yourself – with confidence.

Ok?! I know you may be a bit annoyed with me right now. Did you find yourself saying yes, then no, then yes, etc. when you read that? Take a moment here and just allow yourself to consider the following statement. Not having clarity eats away at your power. If you can see the value in that, then we can look at where it shows up exactly and what you can do to get yourself clear.

Let's first talk about something I call "chasing rainbows." This is so common. What is chasing rainbows? Well, it looks like this: You have a job or a business. You work. You may be successful or not as successful as you want – it can occur both – or either – way. However, you research other careers or businesses frequently. Or you listen to someone else or read about someone else's success (yep, even on Facebook!), and get jealous and think something like, "Maybe I could do that. Maybe that would work better. Why didn't I go that route? Should I change jobs/careers/businesses?" Then you look into it (or don't), but you remain unsatisfied with what you are doing.

Does this sound familiar?

It is like you are looking for the pot of gold at the end of the rainbow. You are chasing rainbows and know, in your gut, you will find that right rainbow... one day. The reality is... that one day never comes. Chasing rainbows will definitely kill your chance of being successful, being satisfied, and being fulfilled.

My experience in coaching people is that when they get clarity about who they really are and what they really want, they stop chasing rainbows and really do succeed – wildly!

The other thing that will get in the way of you being clear or having clarity is being willing. I am going to talk about this, *willingness*, a lot as we continue our conversation. I have found that willingness, or lack of willingness, is often at the core of why people stay stuck in certain areas. If our conversation, in this book, is going to make any appreciable impact on you, you must be *willing* to examine some things, including willingness. Don't worry, I will talk about it in different ways, so that you can examine it. and make a difference for yourself.

In this case, are you *willing* to get clarity? **It is risky**. Clarity comes when you make a decision and a decision, by its very nature, is the act of killing off alternatives. So, when you decide something, at the same time, you kill off something else. In your career or your business, it would look like you deciding on your path, or your goal, and then *deciding* on a plan and executing. No excuses, no waffling, no changing your mind, but doing it, really taking it on. *Risky business!* You might fail. You might succeed. *Both scare people equally.*

If you are someone who has not always been successful – or if you are someone who does not often reach your goals, more often than not, failing is comfortable. You already know how to do that!

You may *say* you don't like failing, and fantasize about being super successful, but, if you really tell the truth, you **are** comfortable with the way it generally goes. Success is scary. Others will expect you to keep succeeding and, likely, will want more from you. That is when self-doubt can creep in. Often, what I hear from people (maybe like you) is that they don't know if they can keep it up. Success seems like an elusive, even lucky, accident and (maybe) you don't know how to keep doing it and then, doing even more.

The other side of that is fear of failing. The risk exists that someone will count on you, on what you said you were going to do, and you risk letting them down. Most of the people I coach hate to disappoint others. It is inherent – even primal – that we want to please; want to be liked, accepted, and even praised.

It goes back to childhood and brain science. When you did something your parent (or a significant adult in your life) liked, they praised you and a chemical cocktail (primarily oxytocin and dopamine) got released in your brain, and it felt really good. When you disappointed your parent, or someone else who was important to you, or if they got mad at you, a different chemical cocktail was released in your brain (primarily, cortisol and epinephrine).

That triggered a fight, flight, flee or appease response – which doesn't feel good. These brain reactions all lead to a *primal fear of failing*.

This "primal fear" is often at the core of a failure to have clarity. If you stay confused or unclear; or if you continue to chase rainbows, you don't risk the fail/success paradigm. The old adage, no risk/no reward is also true. You must first get aware of what is in the way of your clarity and then take steps to get yourself clear. Almost always, this will require giving up your concern for the risk.

I always say (and I am likely to ask *you* this frequently) – "What is the worst thing that could happen?" When you answer that, I will probably ask, "Can you survive it?" – a question to which most everyone replies that they can; which is why giving up whatever fear you have and getting yourself clear, requires making a decision.

It is so interesting how the lack of clarity looks in our lives. I am going to share a couple of stories here; the first is about me and the second is about a coaching client.

I was in a leadership position in my company. My boss depended on me for many things.

I liked it and actually encouraged it, because she was also acknowledging me, my talent, and my contribution (Remember, I told you I like acknowledgement!).

Years went by and I decided I wanted a new position in a different division, but she was now so dependent on me, she would not let me go (or so it seemed to me). How this went is, I would state I was going to go to this new position and she would say, "Ok, but I need you to handle xyz and train Jane before you can do that." I would agree, and I would accomplish what she asked.

Then, she would come back to me and say something like, "Oh, I also need you to do abc, and then you can go." And this went on for about a year, at which point I got mad. As a result, I went to her superior, complaining that she refused to let me go and how she was undermining my career.

What my boss's boss said had me get clarity.

She said, "Why do you keep saying 'yes' when she asks you to do more and more? Why don't you simply state you are leaving and give her a date? If she asks for more, decline."

I was stunned.

As we talked through it, I realized that my boss simply wanted things from me.

I was under no obligation to provide them, and when I kept saying "yes," I was *trapping myself*. You see, I did not want her to be mad at me or gossip about me, so I kept saying "yes," and blaming her for it!

I followed the advice and, soon after, left that position and moved up in the organization. And... she was not mad at me. All the things I thought might come true, did not. Clarity and action bought me what I wanted.

The next story I am going to share with you is about a client of mine. *(Name are always changed to protect confidentiality.)*

Sue was building a coaching practice while also consulting in other companies. She came to me to work on growing her own practice. We went to work.

She was smart, savvy, and a great, well-trained coach, who consistently produced results. She did get clear on her value and increased her fees and income, which was a triumph, but in all other ways she seemed stuck.

However, we discovered that she had a habit; she chased rainbows. She was ALWAYS researching the next new thing and the possible careers she could have; she was never satisfied.

Because of this, she actually grew her business very little. She was afraid to succeed. She really did not want someone to demand her time, so she kept trying to "figure it out" instead of executing. Upon our having further conversations together, she was able to get herself clear. It was obvious that she did not really want her own business – AND, she got clear that working for a company – and someone else – was good for her. Once she did that, she ended her coaching practice, got a job, and is very happy and very clear of her path.

Now, back to you. Do you know what YOU want to cause in your life? In your business or career? Say it, write it down, share it with others, and then create the plan! How much money are you going to make?

Share that; ask for that salary or raise your fees. Whatever it is you want; it is all there if you get clear about it and get in action.

Are you ready to strengthen the weakness in your Clarity Pillar?

Try doing the exercise that follows on the next page: Next up is your Clarity Calisthenics!

CLARITY CALISTHENICS:

If asked what we "do," most of us are likely to give a long-winded explanation or a job title. This does not leave anyone listening with a real sense of who we are or of our capabilities.

Speaking about yourself in this way is a sign of "lack of clarity." So that you can begin to gain confidence and clarity about who you really "are," take on the following exercise.

1. Write out what you would say if I asked you to introduce yourself to me. Consider – as you write this – the benefits that people get out of your work or some positive comments that have been made about you on a job review.

NOTE: In the past, you might have considered this bragging, which had you minimize your accomplishments and value in the world. That is because, sometimes, as children, we are taught not to brag. I invite you, again, to consider that the type of bragging to which our parents were referring was more about boasting; or a kind of speaking that put us "above" other people.

I am not speaking about that. I am speaking *about owning your power and accomplishments*. If I am great, it does not have to take away from anyone or put myself above anyone else.

For example:
>   (*Ordinary description/with no power*):
>>   I am a manager at a catering company and I manage a staff of 30 people.
>   (Powerful description of "who" you are)
>>   I am a rock star manager at a multi-award-winning company where our team is known to consistently exceed our clients' expectations. I have an amazing staff of 30 people whom I enjoy supporting as they grow in their careers.

2. Next, write out in what area you want to grow... either in your career or in your business: Look also in the areas of finance, satisfaction, and level of prosperity; where do you see the possibility of growth and development?

3. What do you think is in the way of you getting what you want?

4. What is one action you can take to make a difference?

5. Write down how this exercise went for you

CHAPTER 3

Is What You Say REALLY What You Want?

I find that there is often a disconnect between what people SAY they are committed to and, upon examination, what we discover they are ACTUALLY committed to. This is a critical aspect of being confident and being powerful. You might ask "why?" this is the case. Whenever there is a disconnect or an inconsistency, and you are unaware that it exists; it can undermine your confidence and your power. I am going to share some stories that I think will help illustrate what I mean, as we talk, now, about commitment.

You must be willing to discover some things about what you are committed to that you may not know, or you "kind of" know, but don't want to admit. Again, willingness is a critical component. You might have to give up being embarrassed, for example, to admit what you are *really* committed to. I am not saying you have to, or should be, embarrassed; but in my years of experience with thousands of people, embarrassment is often in the way of being willing to accept something as "real." So, I invite you to just examine and be open – be *willing* – to discover and tell the truth.

I must point out another critical element when talking about being committed. *Commitment, as I am talking about it here, is distinct from desire, want or wish.* You may want something, hope for something, but when you examine what you actually have you will discover that what you say you want and the actions that you do take point to what you are actually committed to. In other words, your actions tell a story.

When you discover, upon examination, what your actions tell you about your real commitments, it allows you to create different actions so that you can have what you want, desire, wish you had. Examining and being honest about, and responsible for what you actually do have is powerful. That process will always have you in charge of your results and never a victim of anything. When you are in charge of your results, your confidence skyrockets.

Here is what I want you to do: Take an inventory of the results you have in your life. I know that is an unusual request, so I will elaborate. Look in every area of your life; your "personal" life, your business or career, etc., and write down what you have.

For example: I have a husband I have been with for 30 years; I have 2 daughters, a son-in-law and a granddaughter with whom I have great relationships. My husband I travel regularly and love traveling, thinking about when he retires where we might live part of the year and we don't have actual plans or a timeline. In my business, I have a thriving clientele, who regularly produce amazing results and who refer me to others. I write articles regularly. I speak to audiences a lot. I design and deliver workshops. I go out to eat with my friends and my husband a lot. I have extra weight and some knee pain (I could go on, but hopefully that gives you an idea of what I am asking you to do).

Next, I want you to do this: Look at your inventory of those results and you will see what you are committed to. In my case, for example I can look at what I wrote, and I can see by MY results what I am really committed to.

My results, **what I have** (again, not what I want, but what I actually have) **point to I am committed** to a good marriage and a good nuclear family. I am committed to talking about future retirement, but not actually planning. I am committed to my clients and my business thriving, and to contributing to people. I am committed to going out to eat good food. I am committed to training, and writing, and sharing my knowledge. I am not committed to losing weight (because the results don't lie).

I could look at my house, my vacations, my health, my money, etc., and the results would show exactly to what I am committed.

I could say, "Wow, that doesn't work for me!" or "I don't like it." But here is the thing – and this is important: That would be a lie. Yes, a lie. If it did not work for me, or I really did not like it, I would do something about it. I would get committed to another outcome and get into action and achieve it. I know this for myself, without any shred of doubt, and I know it for you, too. However, what often happens when people see their results as an outcome of their current commitment, they decide to take new actions, create new commitments and turn their desires into action. Desires, wishes and wants turn into action will absolutely produce different results. New commitments transform wishes and wants.

Here is the thing to note: Results never lie. Ever. They always point to something. **They point to the thing – or things – to which we are really committed** (or have been committed to). I used to argue this point a lot. I would explain all the circumstances and all the reasons why the results were the way they were.

However, all those explanations were just my sophisticated way of not being responsible and not telling the truth about to what I was really committed.

And, when you tell the truth, you get free. You don't have angst, rumination, loss of confidence, or loss of power and joy. **You are free to change your commitment or... not.**

For example, if in examining my commitments, you could look at my weight. If we were talking, I could give you a lifetime of reasons and they would be a valid argument for why my body and my weight is the way that it is. However, listing those reasons won't give me freedom or power.

The truth is, I like chips, chocolate and cookies. Even though I have taken lots of action to lose weight, the truth is I still eat chips and sweets. So, if I tell the honest truth my commitment is to eat what I like and not to lose weight.

I want to share a bit more, personally, so you can see the contrast between how "commitment" shows up between one relationship and another.

At some point, with both my daughters as they were growing up, we had strained relationships. I worked and worked, and got support and did everything I could to alter that. We have a great relationship now. You see, my commitment was to have a great relationship with each of them, individually. Therefore, my actions were consistent with that, and the results I produced were also the result – and a demonstration – of my commitment.

Back to you. Can you see what you are committed to by looking at your results or at what you have in your life; in your relationships, in your business, in your health, in your finances, etc.? Were there things you discovered when looking at it this way? I hope so. Discovery and awareness are important and can open up the creation of new commitments.

If you want to change something, tell the truth about what you have been committed to and then create a new commitment. The only thing that ever produces results is action, *so get into action!*

By the way, one thing I have heard from several of my clients is that when they do this type of work, one of the things they discover is how much they are committed to being comfortable. I think it is human nature to want to be comfortable. That's not a problem. However, if you want to make changes in what you have, you likely will have to get uncomfortable. Let's talk about what I mean, and what that looks like.

One of my clients, we will call her Sara, wanted to make more money. She took a job at a lower rate of pay than she had made before. She did this because she had been in a situation in her previous company where the environment was what she felt was "toxic" and she left. She had been out of work for a while, so when this new job came along she took it. However, when she got into the job and started working, the job was bigger than she had been told.

She also was doing a great job and getting praised for it. However, when it came to the money, she was unhappy.

At the time, the thought of going to someone to ask for more money, after only a short while in the position, made her uncomfortable. So, on the one hand, there was "I am not happy with the money" and, on the other hand there was, "It is hard, uncomfortable, weird, and wrong to ask for more money." That then was the conundrum.
Both sides of the equation were uncomfortable. The question then became whether the discomfort of staying in her current situation (being underpaid) was worth the discomfort of asking for what she wanted.

Consider that, the worst-case scenario would have been if she had asked for more money and was told "no." Then she would have been no worse off. Yet, if she continued to step over her dissatisfaction by not speaking up, she was likely to continue to resent her employer and her job, and maybe even allow her performance to suffer. Can you see how the commitment to being "comfortable" could have the potential to be of greater detriment in the long run? Think of *discomfort* as growing pains: They only last a short time and the resulting growth is permanent!

In the area of commitment, another aspect I find many of my clients have in common, is with regard to a belief that they should not "rock the boat," or take a chance to have someone not like, not think well of, or be upset, with them.
This commitment leads to a confidence killing habit of stepping over things.

I find that people "step over" things all the time and they regret it later. I spend a lot of time working with my clients to see what they stepped over; to learn the lesson, forgive themselves and move on. It sounds pretty simple – and it is. And, it is not always easy. Simple, yet not easy.

Let me explain what I mean by "step over." In the purest sense, it is what you did not say or did not do that you *knew* (or felt in your gut) you should have said or done. Often the "stepping over" comes from the commitment to not upset another person, or to have someone like you, or think well of you. This, unfortunately, however, *often* results in you being upset with yourself.

Life rarely presents itself in pure form. What I have found is that most people are intuitive and smart. They know there is something they should say, and they hold back; it often is a pattern. The pattern looks like this: They know there is something to say or do, but they don't. Then, they regret it.

They tell themselves that they will say it next time, until that next time happens, and then they don't say it again. The cycle repeats itself over and over again. Sometimes, a crisis happens, and they are forced to take a new action; but often this cycle goes on, unabated, for many years or even decades.

Research has shown that these patterns are actually rooted in your brain and are mostly established when you are young. It is like an electrical switch. When you turn on a light, for example, the electricity flows through it in the same direction, every time. Our brain patterns are like that. Something happens that stimulates the brain pattern, and we act consistent with that brain pattern, every time. The great news is that research has also shown that we can "retrain our brain" to establish new brain patterns. This leads us to the conclusion that we are not stuck with anything; that, actually, anything is possible if we want it, and are willing to do the work to "retrain our brains."

These patterns, also known as habits, are also exercised in the actions you take or don't take. For example; if someone comes to you with a "great business opportunity" and it sounds too good to be true, your intuition could start "niggling" at you.

You are aware that you should say "no," or, at the very least, do extensive research. You ignore that intuitive feeling and say "yes." You spend money, start the business opportunity and then find out details that are clearly a conflict for you. You stop participating. You lose money. You are embarrassed. You are mad at yourself, and sometimes mad at the other person who presented the opportunity. Only, here is the thing to notice; the entire episode did not go well because you "stepped over" that "niggling feeling" – that intuitive nudge. And, as a result, you did not ask the hard questions, did not speak up when you should have, and, you paid the price.

When you step over something, no matter how small, there is <u>always</u> a price to pay. What you step over bites you in the butt, every time. It robs you of your full power. It undermines your confidence. The commitment to "not rocking the boat" is costly and worth giving up. If you can see yourself in this, and it strikes you as an area to work on, I invite you to create a new commitment to owning your power!

In any area in which you sense yourself as "unfulfilled," it is worth taking a "commitment inventory" from time to time.

See if your results are incongruent with what you say you are committed to, and, if they are, notice what you are "stepping over;" change your actions – and get what you want!

CHAPTER 4

Money Makes the World More Fun!

L et's talk about money and you – cash, finances, financial freedom, financial ruin, debt, bank account, cash flow, being paid what you are worth, being underpaid, the gender inequity in pay, asking and receiving the money you want and deserve; all of it.

Here is what I know: Many people have some sort of emotional reaction around money. And it does not matter if you are wealthy, or struggling; the amount of money and your status around money have little to do with the automatic emotional reaction when we talk about finances. If you are struggling, or not struggling but do not experience being free around finances, that may seem like it could not be true. Mostly, I hear from people all the time, "If I had more money, or a certain amount of money, I would be fine." However, what I have also seen and heard is that "more" or the "certain amount" keeps changing. It is like an elusive goal that one can never reach. Worry about finances and conversations around finances, dominate many people's thoughts, concerns, and conversations. Is that true for you?

Here is what I would like you to do: Pause a minute, after reading that and simply jot down your thoughts. Seriously, it will make a difference.

Talking about money gets to the core of most people's survival. Writing down your thoughts and feelings allows you to examine this topic and gives you the best shot at making a positive change in this area.

One thing I find is that most people equate money with self-worth. The media does a lot to fuel this kind of thinking as well. Look at how many stories, both in real press coverage and the movies, portray people of wealth as special. The story line of rags to riches leaves us with hope. Even from childhood, we read stories that portray a "better than," or "sought after" set of characters – who, not coincidentally, appear to be rich. We also cannot escape the fact that when someone has a significant amount of money, people in our society do tend to listen to them as powerful.

Consider that your worth as a person, as a contributor to the world, is not equal to how much money you make, nor how much money you have. The salary you make is frequently determined by a societal supply and demand scenario.

Take, for example, a professional athlete who makes a seven-figure salary. Professional athletes definitely do contribute to the sport, the enjoyment and entertainment of millions of fans and the promotion of products. Yet, is their contribution to the world greater than the researcher who discovers a cure for a disease or a teacher who educates a generation of children? I would argue that it is not.

I know that doesn't seem "fair," and in today's world, it is the way that it is. However, the point I am making is that self-worth is not equal to money. You may need to debunk this for yourself. One way of doing that is to interview people in your life and ask them what you have contributed to them or what they see are your strengths. Often, we make decisions about ourselves, and then view life through those decisions; gathering evidence for our negative view of ourselves.

I have found that, when I ask others, they are incredibly honest. Then it becomes possible to begin to look at life through their view of and gather evidence for their view, rather than one's own. As a result, it becomes evident that when you untangle self-worth from finances, it can really make a difference.

I am not here to tell you to not want things or not strive to be wealthy. Do not get me wrong, I enjoy money – rather, what money can buy. I am all for you being wealthy.

I am here to tell you, however, that until you have examined your mindset around money, and actually created one that serves you, you will experience some degree of concern and angst.

I have led workshops, have an online program, and work with my clients on this consistently. It makes a huge difference. I have testimonials from clients who have quadrupled their income in less than 3 months, had nearly a 200% increase in sales over the course of a few months, have gotten 40% increases in salary, and, most importantly, have let go of financial worries.

Hopefully, that peaks your interest. If you are ready now, let's get into this.

From where did you get your views, concerns, and habits around money? Most likely, from your parents, a trusted adult, your friends, or your teachers, when you were growing up.

Your parents, or some trusted adult, said things about money that you adopted, without considering whether what they were saying was true or not true, or whether you wanted to live that way, or not. You observed adults and friends and teacher's behavior. You went to the movies or watched television. You read books. All of how you view money started there. Most likely, unless you have done other work to examine and transform your mindset, the way you view money has not, fundamentally, changed much over the years.

To do a bit of examination, complete these sentences/answer these questions:

- My Mom/Dad/Guardian told me, when it comes to money...

- When I was growing up, money was...

- What did I learn in my family about money?

- What are my earliest memories regarding money?

- At what age, did you begin earning money?

- When you had your own money, how did you treat it? Spend it? Save it? or?

- What is our family principle/statement about money?

- Did money influence who your friends were as a child?

- Were your friends richer or poorer than your family or about the same? Did it cause you any concern or influence the way in which you acted?

- I believe (regarding my finances) ...

- I worry about...

When you have answered these questions, write out any conclusions you can draw from that information. Often, this is in the form of a statement. For example, you may see a theme, like "I will never have enough," or "I don't want to die broke and alone," or "If I don't save, I will be broke."

Whatever your statement is, that statement is behind your views, thoughts, concerns, actions, and habits around finances. You did not create it consciously. It is not bad, but that "view" is likely not serving you.

For those of you who may want to disagree with that, because whatever your statement is seemingly propels you into action, I would like you to consider something.

Being in action and making money from a negative money mindset can work to have you make money; however, it does not give you any peace of mind. You will be like the proverbial hamster on a wheel; always running from not being broke (or some similar statement), or running towards getting rich – but you will, for certain, still be on that same wheel.

What I am suggesting is that by allowing yourself to examine the statement that has formed your current financial habits, you will find the freedom to begin to create a new statement. This newly created statement will allow you to create new habits. New habits of thinking, of speaking and acting; all of which will allow you to create a success money mindset.

Before we get into creating something new, I would like you to look at one more thing around money that may be in your way of financial freedom.

One of the common blocks to freedom with money is resentment.

Most people have built up some level of resentment about money that interferes with them having freedom and creativity around money.

Where does this come from?

When we are growing up, we are looking around to see how we have to "be" in order to be loved, appreciated, and accepted; to have a place in our families or the world. To achieve that end, we learn to do what, and who, others want us to be. As we get older, we don't see how this has become our way of operating in the world. Most people would define "work" as doing something we don't want to do, in order to be paid. For our very survival, we become someone who does something someone else wants us to do.

We don't even recognize that we are tapped into that early conversation most of our lives. Consequently, we have some level of resentment that grows through the years. We don't want to work at that job – We look forward to the day we can retire – Our society has the ultimate prize; the lottery – We yearn to be independently wealthy so that others can't tell us what to do, etc., etc., etc.

Can you see yourself in any of these conversations?

The resentment deepens as we spend our lives doing things we don't particularly care to do, or we do things feeling like "we have to" or "we have no choice," because "we have to work." This feeling drives us away from enjoying what we do because we see it as drudgery and because we *have* to make money to live. Rather than seeing work as fun, fulfilling, and desirous, we see it as a nuisance; controlled and dominated by society or by others.

We may develop the feeling that we can do it on our own… or we just do what we need to, in order to keep our job or to survive or to pay the bills.

Resentment prevents us from accessing one of a human being's greatest sources of satisfaction – contribution and/or being helpful. Notice that most people are clear about the times in which they were being helpful, and how good it felt; but often, there are certain conditions that have been put on "contributing."

If you really look at it, your work; whatever it is, can be a contribution to your employer, to consumers of whatever you are producing, and/or to society as a whole.

Ultimately, our resentment often has us withholding our gifts from the world or has us sharing them and not experiencing any of the satisfaction that comes from contributing.

Mind you… I am NOT talking about contributing for free!

When you perform your vocation, whatever it is, you are contributing – and you get paid for it! On the other hand, resentment may keep you from experiencing that contribution or it may keep you from doing your best work, because you are just working to survive – all the while resenting it. That is certainly not satisfying! And then, there are the internal conversations like "I can't contribute because I don't have the time or money to do it, because I need to survive," OR there is the mental paradox of "If I am getting paid, I can't contribute."

You may be working hard, but is it from "having" to do so? What would be different if it was from passion and "getting" to do so? Doing what you are passionate about will access your highest levels of creativity and contribution – that is the very best antidote for resentment.

There are a lot of people working hard – very hard – and not contributing anything close to what they could contribute if they were being fully passionate and expressive with what they were doing. Also, consider if you don't get paid for your contribution – if you don't sell your service; people will then not have the opportunity to benefit from your contribution.

The last thing I want you to look at in this area is: Are you *willing* to be rich?

Seriously.

I find that many people like the *idea* of being rich, but in the background, they have some morality around what "being rich" means. It is something on the order of "rich people are selfish" or something that points to not being a good person if you are rich. Somehow, if this fits for you, you may have received a message while growing up that generosity only exists when you are poor – and, that since rich people are selfish, not generous; it is wrong to be rich.

If that is the case for you, I invite you to give that up. It was likely told to you as a way of having you be a generous person; which, in theory, was a good life lesson.

However, having it keep you from being rich, does not serve you. In order to be financially free, you can let go of that belief. There are plenty of very generous, wealthy, people out there in the world – and you can be one of them, should you choose to create it that way.

If you want to have financial freedom, it is time to create something that you want. Here is the easiest and simplest way to do this...

Write down a newly created view about yourself and money. Write a statement of one or two sentences that communicates that view. Then, underneath that new view/new statement, write out some actions you can take and new habits you could create that would be likely to produce results consistent with that new statement.

Make sure that you include thinking habits, speaking habits and acting habits **as well as what habits you will avoid.**

Then, **and most importantly**, how are you going to keep this new view, this newly created statement about finances, from simply disappearing?

What I know is that you must create something outside your memory to create new habits. There is some evidence that you need to repeat something sixty-six (66) times to make it "stick." I find that when people write things down, and create the habit of reading them every day, and if they place the written material where they can see it, that it helps keep those new habits alive.

You can also ask someone to be your accountability partner and support you in taking these new actions. If you do this, you will alter your money mindset and produce not only the money you want, but the freedom you desire.

52 Capable people plagued by self doubt

55 own your successes

56 high achievers tend to focus on what they haven't done vs. what they <u>have</u>

57 minimizing your successes serves no one

△ 57 writing a list of all your accomplishments in the last 5yrs.

57 cease comparisions = an act of violence against the self

57 we often envy what others have while at the same time, they admire and covet what we have.

58 "success is like a vitamin"

58 embrace your brilliance

CHAPTER 5

Will I Get Found Out?

Are you good at what you do? Have people acknowledged you, complimented you, told you how
great you are? Do you get what they say, thank
them and allow yourself to experience pride in being good?
Or do you often think, "if they only knew" or "I am not really that good. They are just saying that to make me feel good;
they don't really believe that." Or, do you see or read or hear
about others' accomplishments, and use that to reinforce
your view that you really are not good enough.

This is so common that in 1978, American psychologists,
Pauline Clance and Suzanne Imes, gave it a name – the impostor syndrome. Impostor syndrome is described as a feeling of "phoniness in people who believe that they are not
intelligent, capable or creative, *despite evidence of high
achievement."*

Generally, people who suffer from Impostor Syndrome are high achievers and hard workers, who live in fear of being found out or discovered as frauds. I have encountered this among most of my clients to one degree or another.

Suffering from Impostor Syndrome undermines your experience of achievement and confidence, as well as likely impacts your performance. It is truly like being in a straightjacket while dancing!

Numerous famous, highly acclaimed people have spoken about it. For example; Sheryl Sandberg, COO of Facebook and best-selling author of "Lean In" said, "Every time I was called on in class, I was sure that I was about to embarrass myself. Every time I took a test, I was sure that it had gone badly. And every time I didn't embarrass myself – or even excelled – I believed that I had fooled everyone yet again. One day soon, the jig would be up... This phenomenon of capable people being plagued by self-doubt has a name – the impostor syndrome. Both men and women are susceptible to the impostor syndrome, but women tend to experience it more intensely and be more limited by it."

Where does this destructive, yet common, thought process come from? It likely begins in childhood when we are encouraged to do our best, but often someone does better. We get driven to be "perfect" and the lifetime of trying to achieve the ever-elusive state of perfectionism ensues. Men suffer from this as well, but it is far more common in women.

Take one example of looking at the qualifications for a job. It is well researched that women won't apply or volunteer for something unless then have 90-100% of the qualifications, yet men apply and volunteer if they have 60% of the qualifications!

Women also tend to be more critical of other women, and thus themselves.

There are other influences in our society as well. For example, it is often said that women are promoted based on their accomplishments, yet men are promoted based on their potential. Then there is the drive to never be satisfied, which may come from our early schooling, when most of us experienced the "smartest" or "best at something" classmate getting accolades, and we experienced jealousy and, perhaps, decided we would always do better.

However, the trap of "always do better" leads to a lifetime of moving the flag of achievement and never getting "there." For myself, I was a good student and got mostly A's. Whenever I did not get an A, my parents always made a comment about next time trying harder – no wonder that I, and likely, many of you, never reach our goals and experience not being good enough!

There is nothing wrong with giving something your best, which is quite distinct from **having** to *be the best*. This drive to feel "good enough" is counterproductive. The mere act of imagining that someday, you will finally achieve whatever elusive goal of perfection you have created for yourself, will keep you stuck and diminish your power and satisfaction.

And, when I look on the calendar, I sure can't find "someday," can you?

To overcome Impostor Syndrome, you must learn some self-acceptance; be realistic and allow yourself to see yourself through a new lens of "good enough."

As I pointed out, giving your best is not the same as being the best. Likewise, there's a distinct difference between trying to better yourself and being better than everyone else. Overcoming the Imposter Syndrome requires self-acceptance: You don't have to attain perfection or mastery to be worthy of the success you've achieved and any accolades you earn along the way. It's not about lowering the bar; it's about resetting it to a realistic level that doesn't leave you forever striving and feeling inadequate. You don't have to be Einstein to be a valuable asset to your organization and to those around you.

Nor do you have to attain perfection to share something with the world that enriches people's lives in some way.

As a side note – about perfection – What is perfect? I assert that it is whatever you say it is, and you are always changing the standard, which leaves perfection a never ending, evolving state, to which you will never measure up.

The good news is that *you* likely created the standard, so as the author, *you* can change the standard!

Nobel Laureate, Maya Angelou once said: "I have written eleven books, but each time I think, 'uh oh, they're going to find out now. I've run a game on everybody, and they're going to find me out.'"

Fortunately for all of us she has never let her fear of being "found out" stop her from putting pen to paper and sharing thoughts that have expanded our hearts and enriched our lives. While she has achieved a lifetime of success, received numerous awards, accolades and a place in the history books, her experience of her achievements was diminished by her own experience of Impostor Syndrome.

Here is what I want for you: **Own your successes.** You didn't get lucky or succeed by chance. It was not a mistake.

You are not a fraud. You did not get away with fooling someone. You are GREAT. Really.

Those people, maybe even you, who often fear being "found out" tend to attribute their success to external factors – like luck or a helping hand.

Unsurprisingly, women tend to do this more often than men, who are more likely to attribute their successes to a combination of internal factors, such as grit, talent, brains and sheer hard work.

High achievers tend to focus more on what they haven't done versus what they have. Take Dr. Margaret Chan, Chief of the World Health Organization, for example. She once said: "There are an awful lot of people out there who think I'm an expert. How do these people believe all this about me? I'm so much aware of all the things I don't know."

Just as we must take responsibility for our failures in life, we must also take responsibility for our successes. *Minimizing your successes serves no one.* So, if you sometimes feel undeserving of your success, try writing a list of all the key things you've accomplished over the last 5 years. I would hazard a guess that even the fruits of your last 12 months' efforts will help you to see how well deserved is all your success.

Cease comparisons. Author Iyanla Vanzant believes that "comparison is an act of violence against the self." Comparisons are always subjective, often biased and rarely helpful.

Our own experience may be that we are working hard, to simply keep our heads above water and fulfill on the expectations of others. We look outside of ourselves and often, mistakenly, assume others are getting by more effortlessly. The reality is that you actually do not know what others are doing or experiencing, and often, they are every bit as stretched and struggling just like you. They may not experience life and their struggles exactly as you do, but they experience them in their own way, with their own unique set of challenges, insecurities and internal struggles.

Allowing yourself to look and consider life from another's point of view, allows you to give yourself a break, as well as bring some compassion to them, as well as yourself. Too often, we fall into the trap of comparing our insides with others' outsides; our weaknesses with others' strengths. The old adage, the grass is always greener on the other side, holds true here. We often envy what others have; while, at the same time, they admire and covet what we have.

The most important thing to do is to examine our own competencies and play to them. One of my favorite pieces of advice came from a parenting book I read and I believe this holds true for us as adults.

✷ The advice was: "Success is like a vitamin; no one pill does it all." In other words, no one person is great at everything. Embrace your strengths and acknowledge your successes.

In addition, this author pointed out that we don't expect our children to be brilliant at every subject, yet, for some reason, we judge ourselves as unworthy if we are not great at everything. A bit crazy, don't you think? Let go of what you think you lack or at what things or skills you think you are not good enough. **Embrace your brilliance**.

p2 clutter a collection of memories from the past of things that did not go well.
"keep memories to ward off any future similar thing from happening."

p4 mental clutter created lack of confidence

clear clutter → developed → new brain patterns for making new actions mistakes

p4 Fail big, fail faster, fail often learn & more on

p5 clutter clearing - not a one & done process

CHAPTER 6

Clearing the Clutter!

I hate clutter! When I walk into a room or a store or any-place that is filled with clutter, I am uncomfortable; I generally want to get away. It is unsettling to be around all that clutter!

To regain your power, you must have a clutter-free environment. What does that mean, you might ask? I am not talking about physical stuff, so let's look at what is clutter and how it robs you of power.

Have you ever had this sort of experience? You were speaking to someone important to you, and they said something like "I don't like that idea," or "Not going to happen," or "That is… (fill in the blank with a word or phrase that you didn't like or want to hear)? When they said whatever it was that they said, you had a severe, maybe even out of proportion, reaction to what they said. You might have even felt a bit out of control, discombobulated, and upset?

Consider that when these sorts of things happen, there is simply "clutter" in your space/your mind, the environment in which you operate.

 Clutter, as I am referring to here, is simply a collection of memories from the past, of things that did not go well. It seems to be quite common that we keep a few of those memories in reserve to "ward off" any future, similar, thing from happening. There actually is neuroscientific proof of this phenomenon, but I won't get into that, other than to note it here.

What I will say, though, is that how our minds and brain patterns operate is that something happens, that we experience did not go well. We then develop a decision and coping strategy to make sure that it does not happen again in the same way. We have all kinds of thought patterns, acting and not acting patterns, speaking and not speaking-up patterns, as well as listening patterns, that keep that mental clutter in place. That is just the way we automatically operate. However, this sort of automatic behavior is limiting. When something unwittingly reminds of us of the old clutter, we respond to what is happening now as if it is the same situation as what occurred in the past, which, of course, limits our thinking, our actions, and the outcome. Let me share some stories about this so you can see it, in action.

One of my clients (we will call her Ariel to protect her ano-nymity), was dealing with this cluttered thinking.

She is an entrepreneur who both sells her services and exe-cutes on what her services promise. She deals with multiple vendors and suppliers from different industries. Her busi-ness was doing well and she was growing her company. However, she experienced having a "pattern" of behavior that robbed her of her confidence and her power, and that was wholly unpleasant for her. The pattern that she discov-ered was that any time she got unexpected news, she would get upset and not be her usually self-confident, great "busi-ness-sense" kind of woman. She would "scramble" to make the situation right or, she would get upset with the other person. As you can imagine, when you are dealing with a lot of different suppliers, vendors, and clients, you are going to frequently get news you were not expecting. This was a bit debilitating for someone running a demanding business.

What we discovered when we looked into it was that she had *clutter* from when she was very young, and her father got upset with her. Since that clutter was there, anything that reminded her of that time, would cause her to get dis-proportionately upset, and would rob her of her power. Once she cleared that clutter, she was able to develop new strategies to deal with news she was not expecting. Very powerful!

Personally, I used to get super upset and lose my confidence when I made a mistake. I was always someone driven to be the best, but I seemed frequently to fall a little short. I won a speech contest when I was young, but then was only the runner up in the school-wide spelling bee. I got A's, but occasionally I would get a B, and my dad would look disapprovingly at me and tell me to try harder. These things had me accumulate mental *clutter* and I hated to make a mistake or even take a chance on not being the best.

As you can imagine, this mental clutter left me with little opportunity to learn new things, or to grow, and left me with a lack of confidence. Once I cleared that clutter, I developed new actions, and new brain patterns for making mistakes. I even have a motto I now share a lot – "Fail big, fail fast, fail often, learn and move on!" which has given me tons of power to grow and learn!

One neurologically based tip I can give you (to quell the reaction), when you do something that awakens that mental clutter (like me making a mistake), is speak about it; give some language to it. Studies have shown that when you speak about it, it calms down the brain's reaction mechanism. Personally, when I make a mistake, I always say "That was stupid" out loud, and that one action has made such a difference. I no longer ruminate on what is wrong with me. I just say it, correct it, and move on.

The question then, for you, is: "Where do you have mental clutter?" Look at the reactions you have, especially the ones that are frequent, and the reactions themselves are often out of proportion or exaggerated. Reflect back to see if you had anything you decided in the past about those "sorts of things' or "those sorts of people." That can point to where you can clear the clutter. You can do this through a process of "completing," by acknowledging the past or what you decided, and acknowledging your behavior and thought patterns. Then ask yourself, "What could I create to interrupt that pattern?" Start doing something; whatever works for you, to interrupt the automatic reactions and to develop new brain patterns and new behavior patterns.

This "clutter clearing" is not a one and done process. I find that if you do this for a couple of months, you will gain the ability to start *interrupting* these automatic reactions… and practice is the key.

Hint: Anytime you notice that some "sort of thing," or "sort of person," consistently irritates you, consider that you simply have *clutter* and take the actions to clear it. Confidence cannot be regained in a messy, cluttered space; especially if that space is inside your head – so get started clearing it up!

67 Communication is the most
important skill set we have
our ACCESS to power & influence

68&69 Climbing pillars of your power

- External communication - spoken word
- Internal communication - ~~say to yourself~~ say to yourself
  self talk
  not your best cheerleader
  completely affects your ext. comm

- nuero science of communications

70 Someone says something -
you hear the words, but you just don't
Hear the words they are filtered
  your opinions, judgements, or reminders
  of something else

70" Then you respond
  not to what they say but to what you
  heard them say. What can you see
  is your filter

△ 72 filtered conv. - intervene
  names of people you don't feel
  especially powerful or effective?
  their filter of you?
  " what are you defending or correcting?"

73 frame - set up context - container
  (glass of ice tea offer)

△ I am committed to ... (commitment)
   I intend to....   (intention)

77 nueroscience - identify thoughts as
   habitual vs truth
   • discover brain patterns fear response
   allows habits to break replacing w/empower
   has its

CHAPTER 7

People Don't Read Minds – Key to Power!

For people, communication is *the most important skillset* we have. Our ability to communicate is our access to power and influence, and allows us to express our creativity, our brilliance, our emotions and our unique self-expression. When done well, our ability to communicate is the key to getting what we want; our success, and in many ways, our happiness and satisfaction are dependent upon it. When done poorly – oh, my! Poor communication accounts for relationship disasters, job losses and failures, personal and professional breakdowns, for wars, for alienation among family and friends, and even incarceration!

In today's world, we are literally inundated with various forms of communication. Information is not only coming to us via personal conversation, but a plethora of media. How the media, including mainstream, written, and social media, communicates their message to us, has a profound impact on our lives. I know I am implying "significance" in the words I am using – and I mean to do that.

I feel strongly that *this* is the most significant topic we need to discuss right now.

If we simply ask, "Where'd your confidence go?" as in, what was the mechanism by which you lost confidence, the answer is **in communication**. Someone said something or did something, or you said or did something, and then you had a conversation with yourself and, "*poof*," in that conversation, you decided something and have been telling yourself that for many years. That is one form of communication. I *could* write an entire book on communication alone. I am not going to. I will talk about it and some areas we will get into deeply and some we won't.

Let's break down how we are going to talk about communication as it relates to climbing the pillars of your power, being confident, and being "kick-ass" as a woman, in business and in life.

- **External communications:** This is what you say and how you say it; in other words, speaking to others. Then there is what you listen to when others are communicating. This whole area is the spoken word;

the observed body language and the tone of voice, both in speaking and listening.

- **Internal communication:** This is what you say to yourself. This type of communication can be referred to as "self-talk," internal monologue or internal dialogue (for those of you who argue with yourself in your mind!). This type of communication can be quite destructive to your confidence and power. I often say; your internal monologue is not often your best cheerleader. Your internal communication completely affects your external communication – more than most people realize.

- **The Neuroscience of Communications:** I am also going to talk a bit about this subject as it is a growing area of knowledge and quite powerful in allowing you to fully access your power and alter – and influence – your communications, long term.

Let's get into this and uncover how to harness the power of communication in a way that has you heard, listened to, and acknowledged; so that you experience yourself as powerful and confident. Deal? Great – Let's get started!

"I did not mean *that!*" So many times, you, and I, say something and someone hears what we say and interprets it in a way that completely alters our intention. Then, we have to spend time, either backpedaling or explaining, or defusing, someone's upset.

It seems to happen in relationships, in meetings, in families, in casual conversation. I sometimes think that it is a miracle we ever get on the same page and get anything done.

We filter what we hear, and we don't know that we are filtering what we hear. If you look at yourself as I talk about this, you will see it. Now, I know that others are doing it, too, but the best way to see it and get powerful with this phenomenon, is to see it in ourselves. What do I mean, filter?

Someone says something and you hear the words, but you don't just hear the words they are speaking. You hear what they say filtered through your opinions about what they say or the subject they are talking about, or through your judgments about the way they said it, or even through what they said that reminds you of something else. These are but a few of the filters through which you hear.

Then, you **respond,** not to what they say, but to **what you heard them say, listening through your filter(s).** Let me demonstrate this.

Pick a person in your life whom you think you know very well. I am going to use my daughter in this demonstration. I know my daughter complains about most things – pretty much anything that doesn't go her way. It could be anything from a simple malfunction of a piece of equipment at her apartment complex or a friend who did something with which she did not agree. It doesn't matter what the source of the complaint; the filter through which I hear what my daughter has to say is that she will complain, that something is wrong, and often dire. Every time she shares anything with me, I hear it as a complaint, or something dire and wrong. Last weekend, I was out of town, and I got a text from her. I did not have my glasses on and I glanced down and saw the words "stand and cried." I got my glasses quickly, and instead of the text being about the thoughts running through my head that something bad was happening and that she was crying – the text actually said, "Best stand-up comic ever. I cried my eyelashes off laughing." I know that seems minor, but truly, my filter is always on the lookout for something is wrong, and of dire consequence, and it completely colors our relationship and shapes our interactions.

So, as you hear that, what can you see is *your* filter?

Consider your career and see what filters *you* have for the people with whom you work; customers as well as co-workers. How does that shape your interactions? Now look at the filters that other people may have about you and how that shapes your interactions.

Can you see why this is critical? First, you have to notice that we, all, are not actually having direct conversations, but *filtered* conversations. Once you know that, you can take definitive steps to intervene; not only personally, but in conversations with others, who may be filtering *your* conversations.

 How to intervene: What I am suggesting here is simple, yet, not often comfortable or easy. For yourself, write down the names of people with whom you interact, especially those with whom you don't feel especially powerful or effective in your communications. Then, describe in writing, your filter for them.

If you have trouble, recall a recent conversation, and see if you can identify what your thoughts were before that person opened their mouth, or what opinion you had, like "Oh, they are just being a (fill in the blank)." Next, write down what other people's filter might be of you.

How you can discover this is to observe whether you can identify the way you feel after a conversation with them, or what you feel that you are defending or correcting. That is likely to be their filter.

Another critical aspect of "external communications" is what you are saying. This includes tone of voice, words, and body language.

The prevailing thought is that words are only 7% of external communication.

This fact creates a problem for most of us, as we rely more on written words than verbal – in email, text, and on social media. When you write something, you must do your best to choose your words carefully. One only has to watch some of the Twitter wars to realize how important this is! I like to think of it this way – I write something, then I pretend I am reading it without any thought. What might I be left with or what questions would I have or what possible ways could I interpret what is being said? Then, I often alter what I have written, until I have said what I wanted to in a way that I think the reader will get my intention.

When in person, you have the advantage of adding in the other pieces of communication – how you say it (vocal intonation), and body language.

If you say, "I like that" while making an unhappy or weird face, the facial expression will be the form of expression most noticed, as it has more weight than the words. So, pay attention to *how* you are saying things!

I teach my clients this really effective technique. When you speak, one-on-one with another person – or even in a meeting with many people – it is best to frame the conversation in a way that others will hear what you have to say in the way in which you intend it to be heard. In other words, it is wise to create a "context" or a container in which the conversation exists and will be heard.

To explain setting up a context or container for a conversation, I use this example: Imagine I have this glass of iced tea and it is a hot day, and I offer you the iced tea. It looks good and inviting and you likely want it, right? Now, imagine I spilled that same iced tea on the floor; even though you are thirsty, the iced tea is not very inviting and you likely don't want it. Conversations are like that. If you put them in a container, so to speak, they are more attractive and inviting than if you just pour them out on others!

You can begin most conversations with "I am committed to…" (state your commitment) Or "I intend…" (state your intention). Doing this one little action will get your communication pointed where you want to go!

Let's now talk about internal communication. Here is the thing – the internal communications we have with ourselves take up a lot of our time, energy, happiness and satisfaction. We spend more time talking to ourselves and listening to ourselves than anything else. We are opinionated and judgmental about... just about EVERYTHING!

You, and I may not say it aloud, but we are constantly talking to ourselves about everything, weighing out if something is good or bad, whether we should or should not, if something is right or wrong, or assessing what needs to change. It is tiring, and yet, we cannot seem to make it stop. It is truly part of the human condition. We can, however, stop having the negative thoughts and judgements *run our lives*. We can, in fact, train our brains to stop taking actions consistent with the thought patterns that do not serve us.

To get into the "how" of this, let's talk about the neuroscience of communication. I am not planning to get too scientific; however, in fact, my plan is to simplify this so that you can understand – and use – this information.

To demonstrate; I am going to share some of my struggles and triumphs. I am pretty smart.

I learned to read at a young age and was ahead of my grade (school officials wanted me to skip 3rd grade, but my parents did not want me to). I graduated from high school in 3 years and got A's in college without much effort. However, for me, every time I did not get an A, I would mentally beat myself up. Every time I heard about someone I knew who did better than I did in school or was achieving great things in the world, I would talk to myself about how stupid I was, and wonder what was wrong with me.

I worked hard to try to always be the best. However, there was always someone better. It was as if I was chasing a carrot on a stick I could not catch. I did not feel good about myself.

I later discovered that I had developed a brain pattern for negativity and judgement. Something happened when I was a young child, and I decided I was not good enough. In my brain, I started looking for evidence of not being good enough, and, as is the case when you look through a telescopic lens, I saw lots of evidence for that decision.

Since this was not good news, I did not want it to happen again, and that created lots of fear responses. In my brain, these fear responses caused a chemical cocktail, associated with fear, to be released.

The release of these neurochemicals slowed down my synapse reactions and did not allow me to effectively use the executive functioning of the brain; thus, I not only thought I was stupid and not good enough, I caused myself to fail by not being able to think quickly. It then became a continuous, vicious cycle that included the habits of acting and speaking that went along with it. As you can imagine, it was a frustrating experience.

When I learned about the neuroscience involved, and understood that I was simply experiencing the result of bad habits, I was able to identify the thoughts as habitual thoughts versus the "truth." Seeing that allowed me to create new thoughts, and habits, and experience my achievements. Pretty great!

I have had this conversation with numerous clients and it has made the same difference for them. See if you can identify the patterns that you go through. It is pretty simple if you look at the consistency of the times and circumstances in which you get upset. You may not ever remember what initially happened – that incident when you were young that started the brain pattern – and you really don't have to. Simply discovering the brain pattern, noticing the fear response, and seeing the habits you have created, will allow you to break the habits and create new more empowering habits.

When I talk about habits I am talking about the consistent thoughts and internal conversations you have; the way you act, what you say, and how you feel. When you are able to see those *patterns* as habits, you can begin to see how to change them. Awareness is always the first key. The next is to create some things you can say or do differently that will begin to create new habits.

This process allows you to take your power back – to harness the power of your brain – and your confidence soars!

CHAPTER 8

Winning Through Others!

When I was a young girl, I read my Encyclopedia Britannica and scoured our National Geographic magazine regularly; all in order to have a window into other parts of the world and those people's lives. Even today, when I travel, I love learning about the people, their culture, what they enjoy – I long to be connected to the others I share this life with.

Now, the world has all changed. Today, more than any other time in my lifetime, we are more connected, more informed with a worldview, yet we are more disconnected than ever.

We are inundated with news of what is happening in the farthest reaches of the globe. We hear about refugees' lives in Syria, we hear about tribes in Africa, life for native Americans living on reservations, native people hunting whale and seals in Alaska, and floods in Indiana as well as all the incidents, both positive and negative, happening in our cities.

Social media gives us access to people sharing their thoughts – 24/7 – their stories, their upsets and their opinions.

People have social media "fights." We have elected officials spouting off "tweets" about other people, groups of people, and businesses. The internet has connected all parts of the world and altered our connections profoundly. On one hand, it is such an extraordinary experience to simply watch this video or that video on the internet and, for example, hear about a young girl's experience growing up in China and escaping an oppressive and dangerous regime.

I cry with her and for her and all the untold numbers of people who are living in horrific conditions. On the other hand, we have lost much of the connection of actually being, and experiencing being, connected to each other. Social media and email often serves as a substitute. People think they know each other because they talk on social media. However, that is **not** true connection. People only show their "public persona" on social media and much of true communication (body language, tone of voice, and facial expressions) are lost.

To be connected to you, I need to really communicate with you.

Also, the true satisfaction of connection, and real contribution, cannot be experienced via social media and email.

You may be wondering how this relates to confidence and regaining power. (See, I *can* read minds – lol!) Well, as human beings, we are better, stronger, and more productive, together – and, I don't say this to be "trite," or as merely a personal opinion... Numerous studies show that when we are connected to each other, we are more creative; problem solving and satisfaction is enhanced, and it has even been connected to living a longer, healthier life.

So, since we are better together, why is it we don't ask other people for help more often?

What I have found is that a couple of reasons are common. One common reason that I hear from my clients is "I don't want to bother them," Or "I don't want to be a burden." Is that what you are dealing with?

Here is the thing about that: First, it is basically saying that you are a burden, which displays a lack of confidence and power.

Or, it assumes they are not strong enough or smart enough to make decisions for, or with, you. However, consider that if you do not give someone the opportunity of saying yes or no, or of offering you assistance, you rip them off from having the opportunity to be fulfilled by contributing to you!

If that is not clear to you: Let me ask you a question. I want you to think of a time when you made a real difference for someone else. You helped them. What was that experience, for you?

What I know, and have seen for almost all of my life, is that people love contributing to others. It is gratifying. Just look at when disasters happen – people come out of the woodwork, so to speak, and can't contribute enough.

It is human nature; it begins when we are children. I think we can all agree that, inherently, people get satisfaction from contributing. So, let's look at the other side of the equation.

Are you difficult to contribute to? Perhaps, you don't like asking for help, you might even hide the fact that you need help; that you prefer to do things on your own, or "don't want to bother people/be a burden."

Which creates a dilemma, doesn't it? We all love contributing, but we don't want to be contributed to. I think you can see that it is pretty hard to contribute to people who don't want to be contributed to! You would have to give up not being contributed to, in order to support others who, want to be contributing!

So where does that leave us, in this conversation about contribution? Just this. I urge you to allow yourself to connect to others, to contribute, and allow yourself to be contributed to; because we *all* need each other's support.

So, what could you ask for? What support do you need? Ask for what you need from others. Take a moment to write down what you need and who you could ask for support. Remember, if they say no, it doesn't mean you are a burden – it simply means they said "no" to that opportunity in that moment of time. If they say no, you could also ask them who they know who might support you. Once you realize how we are all connected, it is easy to see that one person can lead to another, and, eventually, to the right person with whom you need to be connected. It's really pretty simple.

CHAPTER 9

No More Insanity; Change

I wish I had fairy dust to sprinkle over each of you that would have the confidence and power return, without you having to change your current habits. I don't.

Here is the other bad news – people (likely you), by their very nature, resist change. Even when they are not happy with the way something is, it is challenging to change.

Just take a mental inventory yourself, right now. Where in your life do you complain repeatedly about something, while nothing changes? When I talk this through with my clients, who are likely just like you; smart, savvy people, and they see this habit, it is often one of those head-smacking "duh" moments.

The thing that is hard for most of us to admit, is that we are addicted to complaining. It is like we complain about something, often repeatedly, and expect the thing we are complaining about to change. Only it doesn't.

Complaining, as a habit, is rather unproductive. Think about it; you are not happy with something. You complain to someone. You get some sympathy or experience their empathy. You feel validated in complaining. Then you go back and nothing has altered. In fact, the only thing that the act of complaining has accomplished is that you feel validated, and often it has you be *less* productive, *and* you wasted the time it took to complain.

If you do this, complaining, about the same thing frequently, your complaint completely colors your point of view of the situation, and it does not get any better. I have seen this habit ruin relationships, have seen people leave jobs over it, and have seen it completely shut down businesses.

The other aspect of failing to change is that we, and likely, you, work to get comfortable. We strive all the time to be comfortable. It is as though while we aren't getting what we want, there is safety in keeping the circumstances the way they are.

My clients tell me that when they go to change something, the experience is like jumping into an unknown black hole – and THAT is scary.

It seems to them that it is better to keep things the same, than to take a risk on a change that may, or may not, work out – especially when they don't have *any* idea *how* it will actually go.

I will share a story of one of my clients, who we will call Sara, to protect her anonymity. I want to take this from a discussion about it to a real-life example. While I share this example, see if you can look into your life and find something similar in experience.

Sara was very unhappy with the staff in her organization. When I would listen to what was wrong with the way they were operating, it was actually shocking. In my view, it was clear they should be fired. They were taking actions that were costing her business, costing her money, and costing her reputation as well as inconveniencing her clients.

In my role as a business coach, I offer consulting advice, of course, but the real magic of what I do is listen for what is going on with her mindset, experience what is having her act the way she is acting, and observe what is having her produce the results she is producing.

What I discovered is that Sara is extremely risk averse. She plays out scenarios in her mind and, if she cannot be certain that her actions will result in what she wants, she does not act. Thus, nothing changes and she is constantly upset and blaming her staff for not changing. When we talked about it, she could see this was highly ineffective. So, what was there to do? Take an action that was new, and seemingly scary and see what happened.

And, so, she did.

To her delight, the world did not come crashing down around her (her fear); however, one of the staff members acknowledged her insight and got into partnership with her on instituting different procedures. It was slow going, but things finally began moving in the direction she wanted and needed for the good of her business.

Here is the reality: **The ONLY thing that ever produces any results is action.** Talking ABOUT something, is not going to make any difference. You must be willing to take a new action if you want a new result. In terms of taking back your confidence and power, you will have to ACT differently.

You will have to recognize that your current actions are not producing the desired result. Then you will need to experiment with new actions. When you start taking new actions, you will start to produce new results. Sometimes you may have to adjust and change the new actions until you are consistently producing the results you want. The cool thing is, once you do this and change things, you will discover that your fears were unfounded and the next change will get easier.

Let's get more deeply into the "action" mode by talking about *habits*.

Inherently, I believe people are smart and well-meaning, and simply have habits that do not support them and their business growth and success. What do I mean by habits? I mean actions that you execute automatically, almost without thought.

For example, you have thinking habits; like something happens and you automatically think the same thing over and over. Think about some people in your life, most likely either a family member, a friend, or a colleague that you know well. As soon as you start talking to them about a particular subject, you "know" what they are going to say or the attitude they are going to have. That is a thinking habit.

They appear, start talking about a subject, and you already think you know what they are going to say. Thinking habits are a bit like a toaster; put bread in, and it toasts.

Take a moment and write down some of your automatic thinking habits.

Some easy places to look: When you are driving and in a hurry, the car in front of you is going slow or you get cut off – OR your family member complains about the same things all the time – OR you are super busy at work and someone interrupts you – OR you look at your calendar and you have thoughts about what *it* looks like (too busy or not busy enough). You look in your bank account; what are the automatic thoughts that you have about that? These are the kinds of "automatic thinking" habits I am talking about.

You also have habits of acting and habits of not acting or habits of acting a certain way when something happens or not acting when something happens. Some examples: You have your email program open and the minute an email come in, you stop what you are doing and answer it – or conversely, you ignore all your email, and don't answer any of it except occasionally (this is a "not acting" habit or an ignoring habit). Or you answer the phone immediately or, conversely, not answer the phone unless you have a scheduled call. You might have an acting habit of scheduling all your activities and appointments, spending money when you see something you want, or conversely not spending money unless you have it planned and budgeted.

Again, take a moment and write down some of your automatic acting and not acting habits.

The last area I am going to address is your speaking habits. There are things you say automatically, and then, there are the speaking habits that have you not speak. Some examples: When someone says something I appreciate, I have an automatic habit of saying "Brilliant;" of saying "I love you" to friends or family, automatically. A common speaking habit is to say, "I understand" or "I got that," automatically, without thinking and without actually understanding what is being said. Have you ever met (or been accused of being) a know-it-all? The actions of a know-it-all are simply an automatic speaking habit. Then, there are the times when you don't say something, for example: Someone says something sexist to another person and inside you are upset, but you don't say anything, or someone asks you for a favor and you automatically say "yes" when what you really want to say is "No, thanks; that won't work for me." That is an example of a "not speaking" habit. Another one that is common is when you don't say anything when there is a chance is might be confrontational or uncomfortable. You have something you want to say, but automatically, you don't say anything, you don't speak.

Take a moment and write down some of your automatic speaking or not speaking habits.

Have you ever wondered how that habit got formed? You were not born stepping over things. Somewhere along the road of living your life, you started stepping over things. After a while, it became an automatic habit.

In my experience of coaching thousands of people, I have found that the habit of *stepping over things starts somewhere around middle school age.* This is the age when it is critical to your psyche to feel like you fit in; that you belong among your peers and that people like you. If you say something to someone and they don't like it, they may get upset. Worse, they may tell other people about what you said, exaggerate it, and call you a name or assign you to a certain class of people.

The old childhood poem "Sticks and Stones may break my bones, but words will never hurt me" could not be farther from the truth to a pre-adolescent child. If that happened to you, or it happened to someone else and you observed it, you probably made a decision to not have that happen again. AND, the most obvious way to "not have it happen again," is to keep your mouth shut. Thus, the beginning of a habit of stepping over things was born and the brain pattern is set.

Sometimes, the stepping over things habit gets formed when you enter the workforce. You know how it is, you are so excited to have your first job. You think everyone will be friendly and supportive and it will be so great. Then, reality hits. You hear someone gossiping. You are glad it is not about you, but you decide "I'd better keep my mouth shut so they don't talk about me." And then it begins; don't speak up, so you don't get gossiped about.

It really doesn't matter when it began, what matters is that you identify that it did. You now have the stepping over things habit!

I want to get deeper into the "stepping over things" habit. It has been one of the most impactful habits, with which I, personally, and my clients, have had to deal.

It has also provided some of the best lessons and lessons always come at a price. I have learned a lot! I have paid hefty prices for those lessons. What I stepped over has cost me money, time, energy, relationships, and confidence. I am sharing this so that you can stop that nasty habit of stepping over things, too. I am now someone who doesn't step over a gnat's ass, but that was not always my way.

Twenty years ago, I had just left nursing and was starting my first business with another former nurse. We were enthusiastic and had great ideas. We did not have a super formulated plan. We just went to work. We were both hard workers, and we both had a "we will figure it out" attitude. We did well for about a year and a half. We discovered her strengths and my strengths and we used them well. From time to time, my partner got upset with a potential or current customer or one of our vendors. (At that time, she was the "customer facing" part of the company and I was the technical and admin end.) That is to be expected, I thought and I did not say anything; just tried my best to smooth things over. Lucy was single, and our business was her only source of income. I was married and my husband's income was sufficient. So, my husband and I funded the business; Lucy took a decent salary and I took none. I wanted to" help" her, after all, and I could afford it.

One day, we had a brilliant idea and brainstormed how we could change our business. We knew it could work. We began seeking out partners to fund our idea and build the technology. We found them. We had the person who would build the technology and two business men who were going to fund the project for a million dollars. The wrinkle was, that we were former nurses, not high-level business people. They wanted us on the Advisory Board, but out of the day-to-day running of the business. I was fine with that. My business partner, however, was resolute in her objection to this. No matter what we said, she would not budge. We fought about it, and unfortunately, it involved the legal system, was ugly, upsetting, and time consuming. By the time the legal part was complete, I was exhausted, disillusioned and did not want to deal with it anymore, so I killed the project.

In the end, I lost $125,000 of our money, a couple of years of effort, and the possibility of a future financial windfall. Our friendship was damaged and the loss of that potential financial income as well as her current income was lost. Incidentally, our idea was eventually executed by another company, and is a multibillion dollar corporation now.

That was an expensive lesson. I had stepped over all the things that were uncomfortable and upsetting. Had I been willing to talk through them, and get situations resolved when they came up, who knows what would have happened, but I suspect it would not have gone so awry that we ended up in a legal battle and damaged our friendship as well as lost money. (Incidentally, we have had all the conversations about this and are friends again. That is one thing I am committed to – we can always talk it through and not have a problem with each other!)

The brain pattern of helping people, and the resultant "stepping over things" was not exposed to me yet, and I continued to repeat this mistake in different ways over a number of years.

I began working for a friend, who was starting a coaching company. I cared deeply for my friend and wanted to help. She promised many financial and equity rewards, but again, I was not receiving any of them for a long period of time, while she was getting paid. I worked tirelessly; even while on vacation.

I loved coaching the clients I had throughout the year, so I was not unhappy. However, the financial picture kept changing.

She made multiple promises she did not keep. Finally, after about 18 months, I realized that she was not creating anything that was equitable and I ended that relationship. What did I step over? All the signs of her needing money, and being demanding without fulfilling on her promises. Honestly, when I look back, the one thing I know I stepped over, is that in my experience with her, it has always benefitted her and little to anyone else. Another lesson learned.

The final lesson I learned was when I went into business with another friend, doing work that was her dream, and frankly, although I liked the actual work, I was not interested in that professional field. I hung onto her dream because I liked doing the work itself. Eventually, like everything you step over, it bit me in the ass. She walked out on the business, and said she did not want to work with me. This one had me do some deep work with a master coach to get the brain patterns revealed, so that I could finally stop doing things that did not work for me.

When I did the work with my coach, I saw that, out of the first situation I described (where investors wanted to give us a million dollars and told us we did not know what we were doing in business), I created a brain pattern. The pattern then had me live in "I don't know what I am doing."

As a result, I would get excited when someone wanted to work with me, I would ignore all the warning signs and go with it, until, finally, it got me in the end; over and over again. Wow! Was I happy to finally understand what was happening on a subconscious level, so I did not have to do that anymore.

Now, I don't step over *anything.* I speak up. I say what there is to say. I ask what there is to ask. And I work for myself and am thriving. The lessons came with a price; they always do – *and* I learned from them. I have no regrets.

In order to change anything, you must do the work to understand what happened, what you did or didn't do, AND not lose your power. I find simply acknowledging what I did, and then identifying and understanding the lesson I learned, helps me shift from being mad at myself to being able to see what changes I need to make.

The real opportunity of embracing change is that you can transform your new actions into new habits. To translate new actions into new, ingrained, automatic habits will take a lot of repetition.

I have read some recent research that indicates it takes 66 repetitions to create a new ingrained habit. At that point, your thinking has changed, your mindset and brain patterns have altered, and you have new habits! Once you do this, you will have confidence in yourself and know that you can do it again and again, whenever necessary! That, my friend, is amazing and empowering. What do you want to change? Do it now! Change your habits, claim your confidence again!

CHAPTER 10

Crises, Chaos, Distractions & Overwhelm

"**M**y pool flooded. My yard is collapsing! I can't talk!" I shrieked to Carol, my manager. She was calling for a scheduled call; to check in on my progress on a project. It was chaotic. She understood. It took a couple of days of getting the help I needed and it was very busy and upsetting. I was completely distracted and was not doing what I promised. You understand – it makes sense, right? But, although it was justified, the reality was that I **did not want to do** what I had promised, and, since I was having a crisis, *I didn't have to*. I was relieved. I justified my distraction with a crisis.

I have found that often we use chaos, crises, and even overwhelm, as a distraction; all in order to avoid what we don't want to do, or oftentimes, when we are failing. Chaos, crisis, distractions and overwhelm are all forms of procrastination, or the explanation or justification for procrastination. That may not make a lot of sense to you, but it read on… it will.

Let's take each of these states – crisis, chaos, distractions and overwhelm – one by one.

First, the situation I talked about a moment ago; the crisis with my pool happened. Did it happen in order to be a convenient excuse for me not completing my work? No, of course not. You may be arguing that they aren't connected. If it had been one incident that happened in isolation, I might agree with you. However, as I worked through this with my coach. I discovered that I had frequent crises happen in my life. Some were big, like a yard collapsing, and some were small, like a car breaking down and my daughter needing me to get her and fix the situation. However, what these crises had in common was that they got me out of doing something I really did not want to do. I have seen this phenomenon with other people. Is this your thing too? If not, see if any other states or ways of operating fit for you.

Chaos is disorder and confusion. There are many things happening at the same time and it seems like each of them is demanding your attention. Some people describe it as being in the center of a room and feeling pulled in many directions at the same time. When that sort of experience is happening, it is very challenging for most people to know which way to go. Mostly what happens is that they simply follow the "heaviest" or "most demanding" need, which results in letting other tasks go undone.

The other way of dealing with chaos is to do what you are most comfortable doing, so as to avoid the things you don't enjoy or with which you are not as secure. When chaos ensues, how can anyone expect you to do it all? This justification helps you avoid or procrastinate and, because they are "crises," you are rarely questioned. You might be saying to yourself, "Yes, Janet, but it is not my fault that there is chaos. I am just trying to manage inside of this chaos." I get that totally. However, I invite you to consider that chaos happens around you because you allow it to. You don't take definitive action to stop it. To be powerful, you must be decisive and direct with people around you. You must learn to say "No, I am not doing that," and pass the baton to someone else. This is one of the most common things I deal with when I am coaching an entrepreneur who is trying to build and expand a business.

For example, one of my clients, I am going to call Lily, had a growing business. She was doing everything and was constantly dealing with the chaos of having clients, contractors, and suppliers contacting her and everyone wanting answers NOW. In that chaos, she was doing the best she could but no matter what she did or didn't do, she found that she was always disappointing someone. As a result, she felt uninspired and wanted to avoid it all.

This also led to her wanting no new business, which, if someone wants to grow their company, is a death sentence to the business! When she saw that she was actually training everyone to think that she would get to them right away and handle everything herself, and that the end result was chaos, she decided to make a change. She went to each of the people involved and created a new agreement with them, one that was agreeable to not only them, but that worked for her. Then she hired someone to help her and had her set up expectations that were easy to manage. And she started saying no. End of chaos! This left her peaceful, more effective, more productive, and allowed some room for growth to happen.

Let's talk about distractions. In this day and age, with email, social media, text, and cell phones that we have with us every waking moment, we are set up to get distracted all the time. Then, if we look into today's office environments, we have the open space concept and the communal cubes, which are filled with opportunities to be distracted. If you have a home office, you have your family members, and household chores to distract you. It takes real discipline to intervene and stay focused. Distractions are a great way to procrastinate. If we don't create some structures that keep us focused, we will not be productive. If we aren't productive, we won't succeed at the level we know we can.

And all of it serves to undermine our power and confidence in who we are as business women.

What is the solution? Admit there is a problem. Become an observer of yourself and identify the distractions you use to procrastinate. Then ask yourself, what are you avoiding? I find that these 2 simple steps will give you some great insight. Once you discover what you use and why you use it, you will have a choice to do something differently. I am not saying you won't ever distract yourself, but you can control it and choose it so that you don't stay off task for too long.

I will tell you my habit around distractions. I notice when I don't want to do something it is almost always because I can't see where to start. I used to do many different things – from making a call to someone, to answering email, to doing social media, etc. Now, when I find myself indulging one of my distractive behaviors, I ask myself what am I avoiding? Then I play a computer game for 5 minutes or walk outside for 5 minutes. That clears my head and I go back to getting focused. It does take awareness and discipline but the payoff of accomplishment is worth it!

"I am overwhelmed. I will never get it all done. I just can't..."

Overwhelm. I hear that one a lot! When you talk to someone who is overwhelmed, they seem chaotic. Too much to do, so they don't do anything.

Here is the thing to notice for yourself; what overwhelm comes from is a thought that you have to get it all done and that it needs to be done now. You look at a pile of stuff that you have to do and realize you can't do it all, so you effectively throw up your hands in despair and quit working on whatever it is that you are working on.

And it is a tried and true form of procrastinating – after all there really IS too much to do! It is a vicious cycle. One very effective way to never be overwhelmed is to realize this – YOU WILL NEVER GET IT ALL DONE. Really.

If it is all done, you will have nothing to do... game over. You don't want that, not really. So, if you allow yourself to fully realize that you will never get it all done, you can allow yourself to break down the "ALL there is to do" into small pieces, and you can put those in your calendar as tasks. Plan it out. Schedule it. Execute it. When you do it in small incremental tasks, it takes a mountain you cannot confront into simply "things to do."

Trust me – THAT is powerful. Get moving!

CHAPTER 11

Support Sets Up Success

We have all heard the expression "It's like pushing a rock uphill." That describes the experience when the climate, or condition, or what we could call the environment (I will use these terms interchangeably), in which you are operating, is not conducive to your success. There are many aspects to consider in terms of condition or climate:

- Physical climate and condition
- Emotional climate
- Financial condition and climate
- Support structure and climate

Let's look at all the things that might be in your environment that would possibly get in the way of your success. We have already dealt with many of them and we are going to deal with some of these obstacles to success in a different light in this chapter. Here is what I want you to do...

Read the next paragraph – and then, close your eyes. Seriously. Go ahead. Then imagine, if you were living your full potential, what waking up in the morning would be like.

Imagine starting your day. Where would you go? What would your surroundings look like? Who would be there? What would you be doing? What would people say to you about what you accomplished? How would people interact with you when you were challenged or came to them for help? How would your day end?

Write that all out before you go on.

Now, compare that to what is happening in your work life now. Any difference?

Since I don't know your exact circumstances, I will walk this through with one of my clients and you will see where the parallels are or are missing.

*Louisa and I discussed this. And the scenario in her mind was that she would get up around 7 AM and work out. She would go into a lovely office with plush carpeting and comfy chairs around her desk. She would have people around her that totally supported her, cheered on her successes, were encouraging and caring when she was challenged and who offered to help, even before she asked.

She would end her day around 6 and leave fulfilled, with more work to do, but not feeling harried or pressured. Then we looked at her current situation and conditions and climate. And then we looked at what to do to support her moving towards her maximum potential.

Here is what we saw:

- **Physical environment:** Her office was in a cube environment; she had to put on headphones just to work. She felt that she could not concentrate and had to use a number of techniques to simply get her work done. Even with headphones, she experienced being constantly interrupted because in an open environment like that, people just "dropped by." She felt pressed and observed.

  Solution: She put a sign on her cube that said, "Being productive, please do not disturb. Send me an email so we can book time together." She started spending more time in alternate locations in her building and working remotely. If she had a deadline, she would let people know she was unavailable and she worked from home to get done what she needed without interruption. (She discussed this all with her manager, who was very supportive).

- **Condition of Coworkers and Manager:** Coworkers were ok, she said. People in general were supportive. However, she felt she did not get the acknowledgement she would have liked for a job well done. This led to an experience of feeling that she needed to do more to prove herself. She, also, was reticent to step up to bigger assignments which she felt was holding her career advancement back.

  Solution: Louisa talked to her manager and asked for acknowledgement and discussed other assignments she could take on. In coaching her, one of the things she realized was that if she wanted something like acknowledgement and support, she needed to ask for it. It is rare, and lovely when people inherently know what you need. However, mostly you must train them to interact with you in the way that you want. You pro-actively alter the condition in which you work when you do this.

- **Working hours:** She told me that, many days, she worked 10-12 hours and then some on the weekends. She felt she needed to do so because other people in her office did, and she was afraid they would think she was a "slacker" if she did not.

Solution: Louisa talked to her manager about expectations and hours. She got clear for herself that she could do whatever she needed in order to achieve what she was assigned, and had agreed, to do. If she was efficient; good, no problem, and if she was inefficient, it might take her longer. When she understood this, she took stock of her habits and decided to get more efficient. She discovered that she had resented the hours, and often had procrastinated and done unnecessary busy work. When she stopped doing that, she began working much less! Efficiency and efficacy were so much more rewarding!

The point of this part of the conversation (book, chapter) is that your environment, not just the physical climate in which you work, but the people and how they interact with you and you with them, makes a big impact on your power. If you feel that you are helpless to do anything about it, you have no power.

The reality is, often when you take a position at a company, the physical environment is already set.

However, you can still make changes in how you work inside that environment – changes that maximize your productivity and leave you powerfully productive.

Just shifting your thinking from "I have to work here" and "I don't like the conditions here" to "I work here and I am in charge of how I work here," will shift your own power differential.

Another truth is that the people with whom you work, unless you are in your own business, may not be the kind of people you want to hang out with. Their personalities may not suit your personality. Their habits may be disconcerting to you. Their tone of voice may even be annoying to you. If I asked you to list what you don't like about your co-workers, your list might be quite long. Those things all do have an impact on your working climate and condition. Some of it you cannot change, but what I do know for certain is that you can shift how you interact with them, and how those things you may not like, impact you.

Right about now, I know you may be arguing with me... Chill for a minute, ok? I want to share something with you that I think will really help!

To do that I have to distinguish something with you that will seem a bit conceptual and abstract, but then we will get back to your situation and the people you don't like or the things about them that you don't like.

What I want to distinguish with you is a word differential.

That is, I want to talk about what is real and what *seems* to be real or occurring. Let me share an experiment to begin to illustrate this.

There were 2 coworkers who reported to the same manager. One was female and one was male. The female felt that no matter what she said (in email) to her manager, he always responded negatively. She said it occurred that she could not win with her manager and, in fact, she felt he was biased against her.

Her male coworker said he thought this was all in her imagination. He had not experienced anything like that, and so they decided to test out what was real. They switched email accounts when emailing their manager for a period of time. What do you think happened?

When she sent the email from her male coworker's account, saying exactly what she had said the day before from her account, the manager responded completely differently. The day before, when she was representing herself, the manager dismissed her idea as worthless, but the same idea from her male coworkers account (disguised as her coworker)? The idea was brilliant.

What does this prove? That her perception was accurate. Her perception about a bias was proven.

This experiment was done to discover if her perception of reality, in other words, what was occurring as real, was real. However, it is rare when we take the time to figure out if what is occurring for us is real. We mostly assume how things occur is how they ARE.

It is well known that 2 people can witness the same thing happening and have a completely different story about what happened. In crimes, police will interview witnesses separately and often get completely opposing views of the incident, and even of the person. Have you ever wondered why that is?

Consider that why two (or more) people can have a different experience of the exact same event is because of their view.

When we observe some incident, we don't see just the facts (who, what, where facts), we see through the filters of our own thoughts, judgements, perceptions and experiences. That filter, literally, alters or colors, our observation. Thus, how something occurs for me is completely distinct from how it occurs for you. And how it occurs is not actually how it factually is. This is a critical point in you having power in regards to the conditions in your environment.

I will give you another simple example. You walk into a new workplace and they begin orienting you to their system.

It is a highly structured environment and even has a whole color-coded filing system. If you are someone who thrives in organized and structured environments, this new office will occur as perfect, your heavenly place. However, if you are someone who hates structure, likes to go with the flow and be creative, this same environment will occur as stifling and you will not be happy! Same situation, different view, different occurring and different reaction. Do you get it?

Now to tie this all together. When you see that your view is simply a view or an interpretation of how situations occur to you, you have the power to see the situation in a new light.

You can move yourself from someone who is unhappy and a victim of circumstances to someone who is looking at how you can make the best situation out of those circumstances.

When you examine, say, your coworkers (that list of the ones you don't like and why you don't like them) from this view, it will allow you to discover aspects of them that you find valuable and may even like. You have probably done this on many occasions, but not as deliberately as I am suggesting. I know I have!

For example; I met a woman when I was networking, in fact, at many different events. She seemed to me to be "flaky" and "out there." I talked to her superficially, but always at an arm's length. Many months passed and I had the opportunity to view her in a leadership role. Several people I respect had been saying glowing things about her. I thought to myself, "Maybe my view is wrong." When I watched her leading a group, she showed up completely differently for me. She still did the things I considered to be "out there" but that now occurred for me as her personal style, and I ended up admiring her. This is a very powerful tool to use to get your power back in any circumstance where you experience a loss of power!

CHAPTER 12

Confident – With No Apology!

W here we start is where we end this conversation. IT IS ALL ABOUT CONFIDENCE. Consider this quote by Marianne Williamson:

Our deepest fear is not that we are inadequate.
Our deepest fear is that we are powerful beyond measure.
It is our light, not our darkness that most frightens us.
We ask ourselves, Who am I to be brilliant, gorgeous, talented,
    fabulous?
Who are you not to be?
You are a child of God.
Your playing small does not serve the world.
There is nothing enlightened about shrinking so that other people
    won't feel insecure around you.
We are all meant to shine, as children do.
We were born to make manifest the glory of God that is within us.
It's not just in some of us; it's in everyone.

And as we let our own light shine, we unconsciously give other
*   people permission to do the same.*
As we are liberated from our own fear, our presence automatically
*   liberates others.*

Here is the thing. **You are powerful. You are enough. You have what it takes.** If you simply "be you," *fully*, you can do whatever it is you want to do. *Really*. As we have talked throughout this book, you have been climbing the pillars... restoring your confidence and your power.

When you were young, like me, you could do it all and failures did not stop you. Somewhere along the path of your life, you stopped believing in yourself and lost little pieces of confidence. Now, as you restore yourself, there is one very important thing to learn and a habit (that you likely have) to break.

What I am talking about is the automaticity of saying "I'm sorry." Simple words AND they have a major impact. Sometimes, they are wanted and needed, but for most women, they are a costly habit. If you follow many women around (maybe even yourself), you will find they apologize for nearly everything.

When I say everything – I mean from "I'm sorry, can you pass the ketchup," to "I'm sorry, my thoughts on that project are..." This is simply a habit of speaking. This undeserved need to apologize can leave people with an impression that you're not confident; or that you feel inadequate, and are easy to walk all over. Whether you do it home, at work, or anywhere in your personal life, it can be costly. It can cost you promotions, responsibility and respect, as well as salary advancement in the workplace. If you are an independent business owner and set your own fees, and you have a habit of apologizing, this habit undermines your confidence. It is also highly likely to impact your fee structure, as well as your ability to ask for what you are worth; all can be substantially diminished by this single habit.

Ever wonder why we have this habit and what to do to stop it? Well, according to a <u>2010 study</u>[1], published in the journal of Psychological Science, "Women have a lower threshold for what constitutes offensive behavior," which then has them likely to feel as if they need to apologize in daily situations. As women, we are even prone to apologize as a preamble to being direct, such as when stating our opinion or when asking for a raise or a new job or position.

Recently, on "Inside Amy Schumer," Amy did a satirical sketch that made fun of our propensity to apologize. In the

---

[1] http://www.centenary.edu/attachments/psychology/journal/archive/nov2010journalclub.pdf

sketch, various <u>accomplished women on a panel apologize</u>[2], first for trivial things like being allergic to caffeine, or for talking over one another, but finally for having the gall to exist in the first place. Funny, yet disturbing. This completely undermines our power. If we continue doing it, we will topple the pillars of power into a pile of rubble!

Beverly Engel, a psychotherapist said, "You'd think that offering apologies too often is like offering too many compliments – it just shows you're a nice, caring person, right? Unfortunately, that's not the case. **It actually shows that you're not confident, feel inadequate, and are easy to walk all over, whether you do it at work or in your personal life.**"

So, what is the answer?

STOP IT! The constant apologizing not only diminishes you, your self-esteem and makes your voice less likely to get heard, but it is time consuming. Imagine if you did not apologize, but simply declared your opinion, were straight in your communications, and relayed your requests powerfully.

---

[2] http://www.huffingtonpost.com/2015/05/14/amy-schumer-im-sorry-not-sorry_n_7276504.html

Imagine not only how you would change the way others interacted with you, but how you would feel about yourself and your own power.

I was on vacation with my husband in Canada. We were in this adorable little cheese, wine, and pastry shop. We had spent the day on the "apple trail," tasting apples and wine. It was a beautiful summer day and we were told by one of the apple farmers to go to this cheese shop. It was the perfect end to our daily adventure. We were purchasing our wine and cheese treats and were checking out, and the lovely cashier said, "I'm sorry." I said, "What are you sorry for?" She blushed and said, "I don't know. I just say that all the time."

I talked to her a while about this crazy diminishing habit and told her I was on a mission to have women stop apologizing all the time for everything. She got a little sheepish, and she shared how it was really a bad habit and in her experience, it was a Canadian thing – the "nice Canadian" habit.

When I pointed out that, in my experience it, was a female thing, not a Canadian thing, she got a bit excited. She said, "I am going to pay attention and stop saying I'm sorry all the time!" I haven't yet returned to Canada or to her shop, so I don't know if that made any difference or not, but it definitely woke her up. I do that all the time, waking women up to their unconscious and diminishing habit of incessantly apologizing!

Look – if you tell the truth to yourself, you are not sorry to ask for an email that should have been sent to you weeks ago, or for expecting to receive the item you paid for, or for being bumped into on the subway, just as examples. You are not sorry your opinion in a meeting matters. You are not sorry that you are asking to be paid what you are worth. **Confident women simply are powerful in their communication. You don't need to apologize for what you say, what you want, or most of what you automatically apologize for.** State what you want, say what you mean with no preamble.

First, you must become aware that you have the habit. Take a week and write down how many times you have apologized. Observe yourself. Observe how automatic the behavior is and how it makes you feel once you notice that you are doing it. Once you are aware, you can start to break that habit.

Just as apologizing has become a habit, you can break it and create a new habit; declaring your wants and your opinions.

This is what I want you to remember: Be fully who you are. Never apologize for being great. Never apologize for making money. Never apologize for your achievements.

Never apologize for being you. Stand tall, own and own your brilliance. Do not "tone yourself down." to meet the expectations of others. Do not step over saying something, for fear that someone might not like you or might have some sexist comment.

We owe it to ourselves to educate everyone that this is not acceptable. It all begins with you. Be the magnificent, confident you that you are!

CHAPTER 13

You Can Have Whatever You Want!

You have now climbed the pillars of power. You have laid the foundation for that great, tall, big, magnificent life you deserve. What will you create now?

Before we get to that, you need to do something. You need to be complete with everything that has happened. "Oh, boy," I can hear you saying. I am not talking about being "finished." When something is done, we say it is finished. When you are *complete*, you have looked at what has happened, forgiven yourself for what you see as your mistakes and failures; you have forgiven anyone you were blaming for anything, and you let go of the right to blame yourself, beat yourself up mentally, or blame anyone else. You understand at a deep level that the lessons you learned were valuable. You even appreciate it all. Then, and only then, is it complete.

So, whatever you did or did not do, whatever happened or did not happen, that is over. Be complete with it. Be grateful for the lesson. Now, MOVE ON!

Create!

What is next? What do you want to create now? When you have built the foundation of your power, the world is yours. You can create anything you choose. You have what it takes.

I am not saying things won't happen. You will have failures and take "hits" in life. That is simply the way it is; but you have a choice. You can either let those pillars crumble into a pile or, you can stand on them and create – over and over again. **You can do it**.

Own your power! Magnify your brilliance! Be a powerhouse in the world!

Go forth and ROCK IT!

Thank you for taking the time and putting forth the effort of reading this book and doing the work to Take Your Confidence Back!

I would love to hear from you.
You can contact me at Janet@JanetZaretsky.com
Visit my website at www.JanetZaretsky.com

Janet Zaretsky

Free Workbook:

Don't forget! I have created a bonus workbook to maximize finding your confidence and restoring you to maximum power.

This free download is available at:
http://www.wheredmyconfidencego.com